Original title:
Tending to the Tender

Copyright © 2025 Creative Arts Management OÜ
All rights reserved.

Author: Evelyn Hartman
ISBN HARDBACK: 978-1-80581-809-0
ISBN PAPERBACK: 978-1-80581-336-1
ISBN EBOOK: 978-1-80581-809-0

## Harvest of the Soft Heart

In the garden of giggles, where laughter grows,
We water our worries with tickles and prose.
The sunbeams of joy dance on each little sprout,
While squirrels play tag, there's no room for doubt.

With cushions of marshmallows, we soften each fall,
We juggle our dreams, and we bounce like a ball.
The daisies all whisper sweet secrets of cheer,
As butterflies wink, saying, "Life's better here!"

Then comes the arrival of friends with delight,
We munch on cloud cookies and giggle till night.
The shadows all chuckle, the moon joins the fun,
In the harvest of hearts, we're never outdone!

A sprinkle of silliness, a dash of surprise,
With laughter as colors, we paint the skies.
So come take a stroll through this whimsical art,
In the fields of our glee, we nurture the heart!

## Whispers in the Garden

In the garden, gnomes collide,
Hoping for plants on a wild ride.
Sunflowers giggle as they sway,
Winking at bees as they play.

Veggies throw a dance-off show,
Radishes blushing, stealing the glow.
Carrots sing with roots so deep,
While cabbage plots its next big leap.

## A Symphony of Softness

Clouds above are cotton candy,
Bouncing around, oh so dandy!
A breeze tickles the flowers' ears,
While laughter echoes, chasing fears.

Pillow fights among the daisies,
Petals whirl like playful crazies.
Nature's tickle, soft and light,
Makes every day feel just right.

## The Embrace of Understanding

A squirrel waves, then trips on grass,
Nut in tow, with none to pass.
The wise old owl just shakes its head,
Says "Life's a joke, don't dread!"

Rabbits munch on leafy greens,
Sharing giggles, in between.
A turtle slow, but jumps with glee,
"Let's party more, come dance with me!"

## Leaves of Love

Rustling whispers in the trees,
Fluffy hearts dance in the breeze.
Acorns tumble, giggling low,
Falling fast with no more woe.

Fall's embraced with colors bright,
Leaves flirting, what a sight!
Nature blushes, waves hello,
Sowing cheer wherever they go.

## Bathing in Kindness

A sponge of joy in a bubbly tub,
Washing away worries, just a little scrub.
Rubber ducks float with glee and cheer,
Laughter echoes, soaking up the year.

Soap suds dance, like confetti in the night,
A shampoo bottle said, "Oh, isn't this a sight?"
Bubbles burst with giggles, flying here and there,
In this water world, there's kindness everywhere.

## Shielding the Unsheltered

A big umbrella, bright and round,
Offers shade where joy is found.
Pigeons squawk as they waddle by,
Pretending they're models, oh me, oh my!

Cups of soup, slurped with flair,
Hearty laughs fill the chilly air.
Each person's smile, a cozy quilt,
Weaving warmth like a heartfelt guilt.

## Heartstrings in the Breeze

Kite strings tug at hearts so true,
Flying high, with a crazy view.
With every gust, a laugh takes flight,
Chasing clouds on a whim of delight.

Picnic sandwiches with a wink and a nudge,
Giggling ants to whom we can't budge.
A breeze whispers secrets, tickles my ear,
I share some crumbs, oh dear, oh dear!

## The Tender Nest

In the nook of laughter, a nest is built,
Feathers of friendship, no need for guilt.
Fuzzy blankets and pillows piled high,
We snuggle and tell tales that make us sigh.

A tea party hosted with mismatched cups,
Sipping silly stories trying not to erupt!
The warmth of a hug, soft as a cloud,
In this happy home, we're boisterous and loud.

## The Caress of Care

With joyous hearts, we prance and play,
We sprinkle kindness like confetti each day.
A hug to a friend, a wink to a stranger,
Life's sweet laughter can conquer much danger.

In the park, we dance with our silly shoes,
Tickling everyone, we can't lose.
A pat on the back as we jest and tease,
In this whirlwind of joy, we're all sure to please.

## Soft Hands, Strong Hearts

With hands like clouds, we float and glide,
Wrapping up love, there's no need to hide.
We giggle with whispers and share a grin,
Our hearts play leapfrog, let the fun begin!

Tender touch, a gentle poke,
In the realm of humor, laughter's the cloak.
A high-five with flair, it never grows old,
Strength in soft moments, more precious than gold.

## **Cultivating Grace**

We plant the seeds of silliness wide,
With grapevine grins and laughter as our guide.
A waltz through the daisies, a twirl through the air,
We cultivate joy without worry or care.

In fields of folly, where giggles grow tall,
Every stumble and trip turns into a ball.
Like butterflies flitting, we dance and we sway,
Grace isn't serious, it's fun all the way!

## The Art of Gentle Touch

With a gentle nudge, we share our smiles,
In this art of chuckles, we go for miles.
A gentle poke here, a tickle, a tease,
Who knew mirth could come so easily, please?

In the painting of life, every brushstroke's bright,
Each giggle a color, each laugh a delight.
We create a picture that sparkles and shines,
With soft, silly moments, and playful designs.

## The Fragile Balance

In a world of plump and squishy,
We dodge the microcosmic fishy.
Balancing on a tightrope thin,
Watch out for that sneeze, it's a sin!

With bubble wrap to guard our hearts,
The careful art of avoiding farts.
A juggler's act, we laugh, we groan,
Tiptoeing on fragile, funny bone.

## Fluttering Between Worlds

Like butterflies on a windy day,
We flap our urges, come what may.
Here's the trick, don't spill the tea,
Or risk a cat to giggle with glee!

In a dance of awkward spins,
The wobbly giggles, where it begins.
We flutter forth, a group of clowns,
In this circus, no one frowns!

## The Breath of Kindness

With every breath, a gentle nudge,
A giggly push, we all will judge.
A gentle poke, a soft embrace,
But oops, did I just touch your face?

Like puppies tripping over tails,
Our laughter bubbles, never fails.
Kindness whispers, "Watch your step,"
As we slip into this funny pep!

## Sanctuary for the Sensitive

In a cozy nook where giggles thrive,
We dodge the drama, feeling alive.
Cushioned quirks with softest floors,
We build our walls with laughter's roars.

A haven where the gentle roam,
Packed with pillows, it's our home.
With each soft chuckle, hearts take flight,
In this sanctuary, all feels right!

## Keeping Ember Alive

In the kitchen, pots collide,
Spill the beans, let laughter slide.
A spoon that dances with a grin,
Whisking chaos, let the fun begin.

Flames flicker like a silly joke,
As we juggle veggies, nearly choke.
Aprons on, the recipe's a mess,
Yet every mishap turns to success!

## Blossoms in the Shade

A daisy dreams of bright sunlight,
Instead, it blooms in the moonlight.
With a wink and a quirk, it stands tall,
In a world where shadows don't stall.

The roses giggle, a little late,
Whispers of blush, they can't relate.
In the shade, they throw a party,
With no worries, never tardy!

## Rocking the Wistful Soul

A cat with shades offers advice,
"Chase your dreams, they're worth the spice!"
Rocking chairs creak, but we don't mind,
Swaying memories in laughter entwined.

A goat on a skateboard, it's no lie,
Curls in a whirl, oh my, oh my!
Wistful souls dance in a daze,
Making magic in a silly haze.

## Securing the Fragile Dream

A fish in a bowl, wearing a hat,
Hoping to fly like a chirpy brat.
Bubble dreams float, a comedy show,
As a goldfish winks, putting on a glow.

Pillows under a starry scheme,
Catching wishes, oh how they gleam.
With laughter and fluff, we hold it tight,
Securing dreams, ready for flight!

## Constellations of Care

In the night sky, stars are wide,
Dancing like puppies, full of pride.
With each giggle, a comet flies,
Making wishes, oh what a surprise!

Big hugs from moons, laughing so bright,
Cuddling planets, a jovial sight.
Jupiter winks, while Saturn spins,
Asteroids tumble, with giggles, it begins.

Twinkle, twinkle, little star,
Why guard the secrets from afar?
Sharing the laughs with Martian friends,
In this cosmos, the fun never ends!

Galaxies swirl, a playful sight,
Stardust tickles with pure delight.
Cosmic cards with silly puns,
Floating along, we're all just clowns!

## The Gentle Embrace of Time

Time's a jester, watch it prance,
Ticking clocks join the silly dance.
It crushes bread, but makes it rise,
The yeast of laughter, a fun surprise.

In every moment, humor hides,
A subtle chuckle, a playful slide.
Each second winks, each minute cheers,
As we count our golden years.

Time's a sketch with a crayon twist,
Drawing mustaches, a funny list.
With a wink and a nudge, it plays its part,
A clown in a suit, with a giant heart.

So let us giggle as we grow,
Fall like leaves, in a joyful show.
For in this game, we'll always find,
Time is the friend that's truly kind!

## **Raindrops on Fragile Leaves**

Raindrops play on leaves for fun,
Making music as they run.
Each splash a joke, a giggly tease,
Making trees dance, swaying in breeze.

Puddles form with a glinting grin,
Jump right in, let's begin!
Each drop a penny, a playful bet,
Watch me leap, you won't regret!

Nature chuckles with the skies above,
Droplets tumble, full of love.
Fragile leaves giggle and sigh,
As rain paints smiles in the sky.

So let's rejoice in each new sprout,
With nature's laughs, there's never doubt.
For every shower that falls and streams,
Brings forth a world of silly dreams!

## A Tapestry of Affection

Woven threads of giggles tight,
Stitching joy with pure delight.
Each color tells a story bright,
Humor blooms in morning light.

From silly rabbits to dancing bees,
Funny faces in the trees.
Patchwork hugs from all around,
A quilt of laughter, love unbound.

Embrace the quirks, the jolly ways,
In every fiber, fun stays.
With every loop and twirl we meet,
Life's a dance, so move your feet!

So here's a toast to bonds we share,
With threads of laughter everywhere.
Creating joy in every stitch,
In this tapestry, life's a rich!

## The Language of Soft Light

In a world where shadows play,
Each giggle gleams, come what may.
Fluffy clouds tickle the blue,
While laughter dances, bright and new.

Careful whispers spin like yarn,
While silly dreams cause no alarm.
A sunbeam winks, don't take a chance,
Join the light in playful dance.

## Guided by Gentle Stars

Twinkling lights in velvet skies,
Guide us with their silly sighs.
A comet zips with joyful cheer,
Spreading giggles far and near.

When moonbeams laugh, we take a ride,
On shooting stars, we're full of pride.
Gravity's joke, we float and swirl,
Let's all enjoy this glowing whirl.

**Songs of the Vulnerable**

Hummingbirds in tiny coats,
Singing songs in silly notes.
Their delicate wings flutter sweet,
They dance to the rhythm of small, happy feet.

A caterpillar dons its shades,
In sunlit tunes, it serenades.
Each wobble and wobble, each giggling sway,
Turns a hard day into a play.

**Inviting the Fragile Light**

Softly glowing, lanterns sway,
Inviting joy in their own way.
A bashful light that peeks and hides,
Makes us smile, like fun-filled rides.

Sparkles shimmer, teasing glee,
Come out, come out, and dance with me!
In fragile moments, laughter's found,
Bouncing joyfully all around.

## **Echoes of Tenderness**

A frog in a hat sings a song,
While dancing around all day long.
He hops on one foot, what a sight,
In the moon's glow, he's quite the delight.

His friends cheer him on from the pond,
With croaks and ribbits, they all respond.
A butterfly joins with a little twirl,
Creating a scene that makes hearts whirl.

Laughter ripples across the green,
In this joyful space, none feel unseen.
A picnic unfolds with snacks galore,
As frolicking critters come in to explore.

So raise your glass and give a shout,
For moments that twinkle, there's never a doubt.
With frogs in hats and snacks that impress,
It's the quirkiest party, who could guess?

## Nourishing Roots of Kindness

In the garden, gnomes plant a tree,
With a shovel that turns into a bee.
They water it with laughter so spry,
And watch as the giggles reach for the sky.

The flowers gossip, poking their heads,
While ants carry crumbs to their cozy beds.
A worm throws parties deep in the dirt,
He's the DJ, knows how to flirt.

When raindrops fall, they dance with glee,
Spinning and twisting, wild and free.
The mud cake waits for all to partake,
With sprinkles of kindness, it's all a big bake!

So let's garden with laughter and cheer,
Our roots of kindness will always steer.
Join the gnomes with their bee-shaped tools,
In this funny fest, we break all the rules!

## The Quiet Strength Within

A sleepy cat finds a sunny spot,
She dreams of fish in a pot that's hot.
With a flick of her tail, she chases dreams,
While plotting her schemes, or so it seems.

The mouse, quite bold, dares to come near,
Whispers of cheese tickle her ear.
But with a stretch and a mighty yawn,
She ponders her plan till the early dawn.

The cat's quiet strength is no place for fright,
For she's just a lady enjoying her night.
No grand battlefield, just a warm bed,
With visions of tuna playing in her head.

When morning breaks, the sun does gleam,
Our heroine wakes from a whimsical dream.
She saunters around, much to her delight,
A cat with a heart, and an appetite!

## Comforting the Whispering Heart


A squirrel in a sweater sips on tea,
While sharing tales of his last spree.
With acorns in hand, he juggles with flair,
Creating a show that draws quite a stare.

The rabbit claps with enthusiasm loud,
As the crowd gathers round, feeling proud.
To witness this feat of fluffy delight,
Under the trees, their laughter takes flight.

The skies bloom with shades of bright blue,
As a bird takes the stage, singing true.
With verses about love and a silly dance,
The heart's gentle whispers find room to prance.

So come join the show, in the forest of cheer,
With critters who smile and spread joy sincere.
For in moments of laughter, the heart finds a way,
To comfort each whisper, to brighten the day!

**Touching the Ethereal**

In a world of fluffy dreams,
Where socks disappear in seams,
We dance on clouds, light as air,
And giggle as we float without a care.

With cotton candy in our hands,
We make wishes with our bands,
A sprinkle of joy, a dash of fun,
And who knew rabbits could also run?

Through the mist of silly thoughts,
We crush worries with funny knots,
Laughter rings from dawn till dusk,
Our silly antics, a must, a must!

So let's bottle up the light,
And spill it all beneath the night,
For in this realm of chuckles wide,
There's nothing but magic as our guide.

## **Gossamer Threads of Comfort**

In cozy sweaters three sizes too big,
We sashay like stars, oh so sprig,
Pillow forts hold our secret dreams,
While chocolate flows in sweet, rich streams.

With every empty coffee cup,
We make plans, and then erupt,
A juggling act with snacks galore,
Oh look! There goes a flying s'more!

Feathers tickle like playful hugs,
As we spot dust bunnies doing shrugs,
The pets roll their eyes, judging our spree,
While we create chaos and sip sweet tea.

Together we forge a silly crew,
With mismatched socks and friendship too,
Gossamer threads weave laughter bright,
In the cozy web of silly delight.

## The Gentle Way Forward

With squeaky shoes, we march along,
Each step a note in our silly song,
A parade of giggles, not quite in tune,
As we twirl our way under the moon.

Banana peels are lurking near,
And trip we might, but have no fear,
For every tumble is just a chance,
To turn our blunders into a dance.

We scout the land of misfit toys,
This is where we spark our joys,
Duct tape crowns and pancakes tall,
Our kingdom thrives on laughter's call.

The gentle pathway is paved in cheer,
With every laugh that brings us near,
So step with zest, embrace the ride,
In silly moments, there's love inside.

## Shades of Tenderness

In a splash of colors, wild and bright,
We doodle joy with all our might,
Crayons duel in a messy chase,
Creating smiles all over the place.

A sneeze of laughter fills the air,
As ice cream bowls become a dare,
With sprinkles flying as we play,
And puppies joining in the fray.

We wear our hearts on wildly drawn sleeves,
While spouting tales that no one believes,
Mysteries of socks lost in the wash,
Turn into legends that make us quash.

With hugs that bounce like rubber balls,
And friendship that never stalls,
In the shades of laughter and fun so grand,
We hold the universe in our hands.

## The Keeper of Dreams

In a land where socks all disappear,
The Keeper finds them, never in fear.
With mismatched pairs like a clown's parade,
He giggles while making sock forts, homemade.

Bouncing on beds, he juggles with glee,
Fluffy pillows turn into a sea.
He whispers secrets to teddy bears,
In a realm where laughter fills the airs.

His kingdom's ruled by pizza delight,
Cheese castles rise high, what a sight!
With a crown made of marshmallows and cream,
He dances under the glow of moonbeam.

So if you find your dreams don't align,
Just visit the Keeper, he'll make you shine.
A sprinkle of silly, a dash of cheer,
You'll wake up each day without any fear.

## Safe Spaces for Soft Souls

Come gather near, in fluffy chairs,
Where giggles echo and love repairs.
Under rainbows made of candy canes,
We share our stories like choo-choo trains.

Pillow battles and popcorn storms,
In a world where every soft soul forms.
With hugs so tight, they lift us high,
In this safe nook, we learn to fly.

Whiskers and wiggly dance moves abound,
Silly hats make laughter profound.
In glittering bubbles, we float with ease,
Just be yourself, and feel the breeze.

Each heart's a star, glowing so bright,
We shine in colors, a pure delight.
So bring your quirks, your laugh, your frown,
In this soft space, we'll never drown.

## Petal by Petal: A Journey

With petals strewn, we start to roam,
Through gardens of giggles, we find our home.
Every step's filled with joy and cheer,
Though sometimes a bee might buzz too near.

We dance with daisies, spin with glee,
A ballet of blooms, just you and me.
With a hat made of leaves, we laugh, we twirl,
As the sunbeams tickle our frolicking swirl.

Oh, but watch for the puddles, they splatter,
A splash in the shoes? Isn't that what matters?
With muddy toes, we'll race through the skies,
As laughter erupts with each few surprise.

At the end, we plant a flower bright,
A blossom of memories, pure delight.
Petals keep falling, but we hold on tight,
In our heartfelt garden, every day feels right.

## Lanterns of Empathy

With lanterns lit, we stroll the night,
Compassion flickers, a warm delight.
Each glow whispers stories, oh so rare,
Connecting our hearts with tender care.

We laugh at shadows, they dance around,
In a world where giggles are always found.
With cookies in pockets, we share and swap,
Empathy grows at each little stop.

When a friend feels down, we wear clown shoes,
And juggle our worries like silly news.
With bright red noses and playful shouts,
We flip frowns over and wiggle doubts out.

So join our parade, let your spirit soar,
With laughter propelling you evermore.
Each lantern shines bright, a beacon so true,
Together we glow, just me and you.

## Cradling Lightness

In a world that's always racing,
I juggle joy like it's a game.
With laughter bubble-wrapping,
I dance through life, never the same.

A cat in a hat, what a sight!
It pounces and prances, oh so spry.
Who knew silliness gave such delight?
Just tickle your fancy and let out a sigh.

Raindrops tap-dance on my head,
As I sip my tea with a grin.
It's the little things that spread,
Like a feathered friend in a feathered din.

So here's to the moments, light as air,
Swinging on laughter's endless swing.
We find joy beyond compare,
In simple things, like birds that sing.

## Heartstrings of Compassion

A puppy in socks with a lopsided grin,
Wags its tail as it dives for a toy.
Those heartstrings strum a happy spin,
In a world saturated with gooey joy.

A bear in a tutu dancing with flair,
Kicks up dust like it's a grand ballet.
It's funny how kindness can be quite rare,
Yet silly costumes brighten any day.

A balloon that floats like dreams collide,
Gently swaying in whimsical flight.
Compassion giggles right by our side,
Wrap it up tight, hold on to the light!

So let's wear our heart like an oversized hat,
And share silly dance-offs without a care.
With bright colors splashed in the chat,
In the laughter, we're all the same fare.

## **Blossoms of Hope**

A garden of giggles blooms by the door,
With daisies wearing spectacles, quite the scene.
They whisper jokes that we can't ignore,
And tickle the soil with a twinkling sheen.

Butterflies flutter like confetti in flight,
Tickling our noses, oh what a treat!
They flutter their wings, full of delight,
Dancing with joy through the summer heat.

Frogs wearing crowns throw a grand ball,
Their croaks sound like laughter in the night.
Join in their fun, let your inhibitions fall,
As blossoms of hope fill the world with light.

So plant your thoughts in the soil of cheer,
And water them with smiles every day.
Each bloom that grows will sparkle and sear,
Sowing the seeds of laughter in a funny way.

## **Feather-Light Moments**

A feather floats down like a whispering sigh,
Tickling your nose as it drifts in the breeze.
It dances in circles, oh so spry,
To a tune only joy can seize.

Knock-knock jokes from the squirrels in the trees,
Bouncing between branches, they dart and dive.
With laughter that jingles, they teeter with ease,
Each chuckle a spark that keeps us alive.

Clouds in pajamas drift slowly above,
While sunshine giggles, tickling the ground.
In these moments we cherish, take hold of love,
For feather-like laughter is truly profound.

So let's leap like kangaroos, knee-deep in fun,
Every hop is a blessing, a joyous retreat.
With each silly moment, we shine like the sun,
Finding joy in the lightness beneath our feet.

## Comfort in Vulnerability

In a world of wobbling jelly,
We dance on toes so silly.
With hearts as soft as marshmallow fluff,
We giggle, 'Is this enough?'

A stumble here, a trip over there,
But laughter fills the air.
With each misstep, we find delight,
Our woes forgotten in the light.

Whispers of worries, we toss aside,
Like old shoes we no longer ride.
In the mess, we find our grace,
What a joy to embrace this space!

Through the awkward, rollicking ride,
We bounce and shake, nowhere to hide.
With every fumble, our spirits lift,
In this comedy, we find our gift.

## Delicate Embrace

Like kittens tangled in a yarn,
We wrap our hearts in gentle charm.
With silly grins and softened eyes,
We find our rhythm in surprise.

A hug that's more like a clumsy fall,
We laugh and bounce against the wall.
In every squish and cuddle tight,
We spin in joy, hearts feeling light.

The art of being slightly awkward,
Turns each moment into treasure.
With every squeeze, a chuckle shared,
A dance of warmth, none can be scared.

So here we lie, all limbs entwined,
Finding love, the softest kind.
In these delicate, funny ways,
We bloom like flowers on sunny days.

## The Language of Softness

In a world where words might clash,
We speak in giggles and a bash.
With every chuckle, a silent cheer,
Our language floats, so light and clear.

Comfy socks and pillow fights,
Turning grumbles into delights.
In the whispers shared at night,
We find our heart's purest light.

Tickle wars and silly grins,
In the chaos, joy begins.
Navigating through life's haze,
We laugh and dance in funny ways.

No need for worry, no time to fear,
In our softness, all is cheer.
With each soft touch, the world feels right,
We write our tales in giggles bright.

## Harmonies of Healing

In a concert of hiccups and snorts,
We find our way, the best of sorts.
With off-key tunes and flailing arms,
Who knew that chaos had its charms?

Twirling softly on our toes,
With every misstep, laughter flows.
In every note that might go wrong,
We create our quirky, happy song.

Joining hands with slaps and bumps,
We find the rhythm in life's pumps.
With every pratfall, we sing out loud,
In this crazy place, we feel so proud.

So grab a friend, and join the spree,
In each soft note, we're wild and free.
With giggles rising like a prayer,
Together healed, beyond compare.

## A Quilt of Gentle Reminders

Stitching worries like a quilt,
Each patch a giggle, joy built.
A little note said, "Take a break,"
While sipping tea and a big slice of cake.

Feelings float like bits of fluff,
Tickling noses, oh so tough.
Laughter wraps around us tight,
As we dance under the moonlight.

A sprinkle of humor, a dash of cheer,
Reminding us of what we hold dear.
With every laugh, the world seems bright,
Woven warmth in the cool twilight.

So here's a quilt for all to wear,
With funny patches free from care.
Let's mend our hearts with a hearty grin,
And invite the joy that lives within.

## **Fragile Yet Fierce**

She walks with grace, yet slips on ice,
A tumble here, but isn't it nice?
Fragile heart, fierce as a bear,
Watch out world—she's got flair!

With every faux pas, a lesson learned,
In awkward moments, our laughter churned.
Like a clumsy cat in a fancy hat,
Who knew being goofy was where it's at?

She juggles joy and mess like a pro,
Falling in love—on the floor, oh no!
Yet fierce she stands, with laughter loud,
In her silly mishaps, we're all so proud.

So let us toast to the absurd, dear friend,
May we all embrace each slip, each bend.
For fragile hearts are fierce, it's true,
And laughter's the glue that bonds me and you.

## Echoes of the Heart

Whispers float on the breeze of fate,
Voices chuckle as we navigate.
Each heartbeat's a rhythm, silly and sweet,
In the dance of life, we laugh on our feet.

Echoes bounce from wall to wall,
"Incredible muffin!" we merrily call.
When love feels like juggling, we drop a pie,
But somehow come back with a wink and a sigh.

Let's sing our tunes in a comical way,
With missteps and giggles, we'll dance and play.
The heart finds its echo in laughter's embrace,
And we chase our reflections in this joyful race.

So gather round, let puns take flight,
In echoes of joy, we'll ignite the night.
With humor in pockets, we'll roam near and far,
Creating memories—the best kind of bizarre.

## Embracing the Wounded

With open arms and a goofy grin,
Let's wrap our worries in a silly spin.
A band-aid here, for laughter there,
We'll heal the bruises with love and care.

Like sticky notes on a wayward fridge,
We bring the humor, a bright little bridge.
When times get tough, we trip and slide,
But with every laugh, there's nothing to hide.

Join in the fun of patchwork hearts,
Finding the joy in all the parts.
Lives entangled in a dance so grand,
We'll embrace each wound—oh isn't it planned?

For friendships flourish when humor's in sight,
We'll twirl through the shadows, embracing the light.
A circle of laughter to mend and defend,
In this crazy journey, we're all the best friend.

## Cherishing the Fragile

In a world so wild and wacky,
We dance with things that feel a bit tacky.
A cactus with a heart of gold,
Whispers secrets never told.

With a cup that sings and laughs,
Balance it all, or face the gaffs.
Tiptoe softly, don't break the stew,
For even glue needs a hug, it's true!

When a biscuit crumbles with glee,
Rejoice, for it's a jubilant spree.
Snuggled in crumbs, we giggle wide,
Embracing all, with hilarious pride.

So here's to the quirks of the frail,
May they make us laugh, never pale.
For life's too short to tread like a pro,
Let's sprinkle some joy, let the laughter grow!

## Alchemy of Affection

In the lab of love, we mix and blend,
Take a pinch of joy, and let it extend.
Stirring kindness, oh what a sight,
Turning frowns into sparks of delight.

A dash of giggles, a splash of cheer,
Pouring out warmth, like a hot cup of beer.
Mixing the weird with the sweet and the sour,
Creating a potion that blooms like a flower.

With each heartbeat, we shake and quake,
It's science, no doubt, make no mistake.
Transforming the mundane into the sublime,
Like turning stale bread into laughter and rhyme.

So join the dance of the odd and the fun,
Let's celebrate life till the day is done.
For affection's magic is wild and free,
A bubbling cauldron of pure jubilee!

## Woven with Compassion

In a fabric shop of silly threads,
We weave our hearts, where laughter spreads.
A patchwork quilt of giggles and grace,
Stitching smiles on every face.

With threads of kindness, we create,
Patterns of love that can't abate.
Sometimes it's crazy, sometimes it's wild,
But in this mess, we've all beguiled.

Each loop a story, each knot a cheer,
A tapestry bright, so crystal clear.
When life unravels, just tie a bow,
For even the frayed can put on a show.

So weave away, with joy on display,
Let humor dance and lead the way.
For in this fabric of hilarious delight,
Compassion shines oh-so-brightly, so bright!

## The Art of Gentle Care

In a world unbending, I tiptoe with flair,
Caring for whispers as light as the air.
A cupcake's frosting? Don't hold it too tight,
Or it'll squish down and give quite a fright!

With gentle hands, we carry the bliss,
Cradling moments that we don't want to miss.
Let's sprinkle confetti on pancakes and toast,
For laughter with breakfast, we surely can boast!

When cupcakes wobble like jelly on glee,
Hold with a chuckle, don't lose your spree.
For laughter's the key, with icing to share,
The art of soft moments, we all must declare!

So let's embrace the giggles and fun,
With every soft tickle, we're never outdone.
Gentle care's not just sweet, it's a blast,
A gift we can cherish, unsurpassed!

## The Quilt of Compassion

Stitching laughter in the seams,
Patchwork dreams filled with gleams.
A laugh so loud, it shakes the thread,
Who knew kindness could be widespread?

Pigeons dance as I thread the reel,
With every loop, I turn the wheel.
Making warmth, not just a cover,
A quilt that makes all grumpy hearts hover!

Each square a hug, each stitch a cheer,
Together we laugh, each far and near.
Sewing joy with a side of flair,
Creating smiles without compare!

So grab a patch, join the plot,
In this dandy quilt, who cares if it's hot?
Laughter woven in every fold,
A patchwork tale of kindness bold!

## The Nourishing Path

Follow the crumbs of giggly glee,
A trail of donuts, come dance with me!
Each step we take is filled with fun,
Like chasing sunshine, we're never done!

With sprinkles here and syrup there,
We bounce through life without a care.
Cupcakes smiling at every glance,
With every bite, we skip and prance!

Banana peels underfoot provide,
An opportunity to slip and slide.
With every chuckle, our hearts expand,
On this silly path, let's make a stand!

So grab your fork, don't be shy,
Join the feast of giggles that fly.
On the path where joy is the crown,
Let's munch and crunch, and never frown!

## Gentle Seeds of Rebirth

Throw the seeds of silly grace,
In the garden of a goofy place.
Watch them sprout with quirky flair,
Growing giggles everywhere!

The daisies wear tiny hats and ties,
Winking at bees that dance and fly.
With every bloom, a chuckle grows,
In this jolly land where laughter flows!

Water with jokes and sunshine bright,
Morning glories soaking up delight.
In every corner, glee takes flight,
Dancing together, what a sight!

So let's plant joy, with love and cheer,
Tend this garden all through the year.
For in this space, we laugh and play,
Growing seeds of joy every day!

## Hearts Wrapped in Warmth

Wrap your heart in fuzzy hugs,
With silly socks and pickle jugs.
A cozy space where moot meets fun,
Under the blanket of a golden sun!

Juggling hearts, mittens in tow,
Making snowballs to toss, oh no!
Each giggle rolls like fluffy snow,
Creating warmth wherever we go!

So gather round, let's light the fire,
With marshmallows of laughter, we'll never tire.
In this place, we rub our toes,
With hearts wrapped tight, our love just grows!

So dance and twirl, let's not be shy,
In this warm cocoon, we can surely fly.
With every laugh, our spirits sway,
Under this warmth, we choose to play!

**Emotions in Bloom**

In gardens where giggles grow,
Petals dance in a breezy show.
Flowers wear their hats askew,
Whispering secrets, just a few.

A daisy trips over its lace,
While roses blush with a smiley face.
Butterflies chuckle in delight,
As sunbeams play hide and seek each night.

Bumblebees buzz out a tune,
While daisies hum a light monsoon.
Laughter sprouts from the ground's embrace,
In this floral, funny, vibrant space.

So gather 'round, don't be a bore,
Join the blooms, let your spirit soar!
In petals and smiles, we conjure cheer,
As nature broadcasts her giggle here.

## Finding Strength in Softness

Soft marshmallows take a stance,
In a pillow fight, they prance.
Cotton clouds puff out their chests,
Claiming strength with cozy jest.

Feathers fluffed in a pillow war,
Each 'thwack' earns a playful score.
The gentler wins in this great race,
With laughs that fill the playful space.

Even the feathers know the game,
They giggle softly, never the same.
Who knew that delicate could defy?
As gentle hearts reach for the sky!

So let your heartache find release,
Through laughter, joy, and sweet caprice.
In every soft embrace and cheer,
Strength is found when you hold near.

## **Nurturing Whispers**

Whispers of wind in the trees,
Tickling leaves with a gentle tease.
A squirrel chuckles, with acorn in hand,
Telling tales that tickle the land.

Breezes weave through daisies tall,
While butterflies leap, never to fall.
Every flower wears a knowing grin,
As secrets of laughter swirl and spin.

In the hush of twilight's embrace,
Night critters join the goofy race.
Crickets chirp in a comic spree,
Under the moon's light-hearted glee!

So listen close, and you will hear,
Nature's whispers, full of cheer.
Each giggle carries far and wide,
In the harmony that blooms inside.

## Gentle Hands on Fragile Blooms

With gentle hands, we weave a rhyme,
Pinky promises, not for a crime.
Petals giggle under our sway,
As clumsy fingers find their way.

Frilly fronds shake in delight,
With every tickle through the night.
Sunshine giggles on each green leaf,
As nature chuckles, free from grief.

A bouquet fumbles with its charm,
Punchlines hide in the blooming calm.
Fragile blooms, tough in their guise,
Wink at us with knowing eyes.

So gather close, let laughter bloom,
In this garden of whimsical gloom.
With gentle hands, we nurture fun,
Under the laughter of the setting sun.

## **In the Arms of Kindness**

Baking cookies in a storm,
Trying to keep my cat warm.
Flour flies like confetti,
Who knew baking could be so petty?

A hug from a friend, oh what a sight,
It makes the darkest days so bright.
Like squirrels at play in the park,
Kindness is a joy—purely off the chart!

A dance with the broom, I trip and I spin,
Chasing my dog—do I dare to win?
Each laugh a drop of cheer so sweet,
In this chaos, I find my beat.

A heart-shaped pancake on a plate,
A breakfast feast that just can't wait.
With each silly gesture that life sends my way,
I smile and dance—life's funny ballet!

## Sowing Seeds of Serenity

In a garden of giggles, I plant my dreams,
Watering hopes with silly screams.
A seed that burps and a flower that farts,
Nature's laughter—a tickle in my heart.

My gnomes wear shades, chilling on the lawn,
Pondering life as the sunlight's drawn.
They gossip about the squirrel's grand schemes,
Turning the mundane to whimsical themes.

With every weed pulled, a chuckle I find,
Two rabbits debating—who's the best kind?
The carrots roll away from their stew,
In this garden of laughter, life feels brand new.

Banana peels scattered, oh what a sight,
Slipping and sliding, I learn to take flight.
With each silly stumble, the joy doesn't wane,
In my patch of peace, I dance in the rain!

## The Rhythm of Nurture

With a pot and a plant, I groove to the beat,
Singing soft tunes while I dance on my feet.
The leaves sway gently to my silly song,
In the world of nurture, where we all belong.

Each water drop a note in my melody,
A rhythm of joy in the great symphony.
The sun joins in, casting shadows so wide,
We waltz through the day, with nature as our guide.

A caterpillar wiggles, a sweet little ska,
Bringing laughter, like a warm cup of cha.
With each tiny sprout, my heart takes a leap,
In this dance of growth, there's joy to keep.

From daisies to dandelions, a parade of delight,
Twisting and turning, we sway in the light.
In the garden of giggles, we nurture with glee,
Creating a world that sings, "Just let it be!"

## Shadows of Loving

My shadow's a dancer, twirling with flair,
Jumps behind me, fills the morning air.
In the world of loving, we're goofy and bright,
Chasing each other—what a delightful sight!

The moon joins along, casting playful shapes,
While I trip over shoes and escape the drapes.
Laughter follows close, like a dog on a run,
In this silly dance, we've already won.

There's a cactus in love, wearing skyscraper shoes,
Sending hugs to a snail—oh, what funny views!
Each odd couple shows love in a twist,
In shadows of caring, nothing's amiss.

A floating balloon whispers jokes to the sun,
While I tumble in giggles, laughing so fun!
In this shadowy dance, we find joy so grand,
With love as our guide, we'll forever hand in hand!

## Beneath the Willow's Whisper

Beneath the willow, I took a nap,
While squirrels held a dance, what a trap!
They wore tiny hats, and shook their tails,
With acorns in hand, telling tall tales.

A gentle breeze teased my lazy feet,
Tickling my toes, oh what a feat!
I laughed out loud, causing ducks to quack,
One wobbled over, 'Get back on track!'

The sun peeked out, a cheeky glow,
Giggling along, it put on a show.
The shade danced lightly, a wiggly sway,
While I just lay there, enjoying the play.

Oh, life's a picnic under trees' embrace,
Each moment a jest, with laughter to chase.
The willow grinned; I'm sure it agreed,
That merriment blooms in nature's seed.

## Seeds of Warmth

In the garden where giggles unfold,
Seeds of warmth sprout like treasure untold.
A tomato laughed, 'I'm ripe for the dance!'
While radishes blushed in a leafy romance.

Sunflowers winked with petals of gold,
Spreading cheer, as stories are told.
A worm in a cape, with goggles and flair,
Wriggled around without a single care.

The carrots wore glasses, reading the ground,
Bantering on, as friendship was found.
The lettuce rejoiced, 'Let's have a feast!'
As veggies hummed tunes, to say the least!

So we gathered our giggles and shared a bite,
In this garden, every moment feels right.
With seeds of warmth sown deep in our hearts,
Laughter blooms bright; life's true works of art.

## **Veils of Tenderness**

In a world wrapped in veils of delight,
Came a pancake flipped with all of its might.
It spun through the air, a fluffy surprise,
Landing right on a friend's unsuspecting eyes.

Jellybeans giggled, all colors in line,
Swaying to music, oh how they shine!
Marshmallows chimed in, 'Let's start a parade,'
With whipped cream crowns, a sweet crusade.

Cotton candy floated, all pink and absurd,
Shouting, 'Join us!' in whispers, unheard.
While chocolate danced wildly in creamy delight,
Spreading sweetness, oh what a sight!

So behold the magic in every small jest,
Veils of kindness that truly are best.
With laughter as frosting on life's tasty cake,
Every moment of joy is ours to partake.

## Surrender to Sweetness

In the land of cakes where whispers collide,
I surrendered to sweetness, it's hard to hide.
Cupcakes in tutus twirled round the room,
While cookies conspired with chocolatey gloom.

The licorice kept stealing the scene,
With jellybean cheers, living the dream.
A donut declared, 'I'm the star of the day!'
While muffins rolled out for a sugary play.

Sprinkles threw confetti, a colorful spree,
As cherries bounced in a nutty jubilee.
The frosting looked on, proud as can be,
'In this circus of flavor, we all run free!'

So let loose your giggles and relish the fun,
In this realm of sweetness, there's room for everyone.
For life is a banquet, a sugary blend,
And laughter, my friends, is the best kind of friend.

## Refuge for the Heartfelt

In a blanket of giggles, we hide,
With laughter as our cozy guide.
Let's build a fort of silly dreams,
Where nothing's ever as it seems.

Handshakes made of silly string,
Chasing joy like a wobbly king.
Our hearts in dance, a bouncy tune,
Sipping nectar from a plastic spoon.

Stories wrapped in bubble gum,
Tickling fancies, here they come!
In this silly space, we're free,
Embracing warmth, just you and me.

So grab your giggles, don't retreat,
In this haven, life's a treat.
Let's craft the odd, the quirky, the bright,
In our patterned patchwork, all feels right.

## Sowing Comfort in the Storm

Puddles splash with each small leap,
While clouds above begin to weep.
With umbrellas turned to dainty hats,
We dance through raindrops, just like cats.

A storm of giggles breaks the night,
As lightning draws a silly light.
We harvest joy from every crack,
With splashes, we'll never look back.

Holding hands, we skip and glide,
Each rain drip brings a wobbly ride.
A sprinkle here, a drizzle there,
My heart's umbrella's love to share.

Together we'll weather any tease,
With laughter growing like tall trees.
In storms we find our brightest hue,
With comfort sewn in shades of you.

## The Rhythm of Gentle Echoes

In the hallway, whispers waltz,
With giggles popping like a pulse.
A melody of quirky charms,
We dance around in silly arms.

Echoes bounce from wall to wall,
Silly sounds make our spirits sprawl.
With every twist, we can't resist,
The wiggles in our hearts persist.

Each heartbeat sings a funny tune,
Blending joy with a silver spoon.
In playful steps, we feel the beat,
A rhythm of happiness feels sweet.

So step along the lined-up floor,
Let every giggle unlock the door.
With soothing sounds of the absurd,
The echoes laugh with every word.

## Lullaby for the Souls

A pillow made of marshmallow fluff,
Sings a song that's sweet, not tough.
With every yawn, a chuckle springs,
In dreams of kittens, our laughter sings.

Stars are winking with playful grins,
As sleepy heads drift where joy begins.
Snuggling in a happy cloud,
Whispers float, soft and loud.

A lullaby of goofy rhymes,
Tickling hearts with silly chimes.
In snoozing dreams where wonders wake,
We find the comfort, giggles make.

So close your eyes to soft delights,
As laughter dances through the night.
In every breath, a spark ignites,
With night's gentle hugs, our joy takes flight.

## The Palette of Sincerity

With colors bright and shades so bold,
I paint my feelings, truth be told.
Each brushstroke giggles, laughter spills,
While clumsy swirls reveal my thrills.

A canvas filled with silly dreams,
Where sunshine dances, or so it seems.
But watch your step, avoid the mess,
For paint in hair can cause distress!

I'll splash some hues of pure delight,
Then watch my cat decide to fight.
She leaps and lands on every hue,
Now I'm a rainbow too, who knew?

So let's embrace this artsy spree,
With splatters, giggles, just you and me.
A palette made of joy and fun,
In our creative world, we're never done!

## Embracing the Sensitive Soul

The gentle heart with tender flair,
Wears every feeling like a rare heir.
With socks that clash and hats askew,
It struts around, a vibrant view.

When laughter flies like kites in spring,
The sensitive soul can feel the sting.
A sneeze can echo like a bomb,
Yet giggles follow, sweet as calm.

They dance through life with awkward grace,
And break the rules in every space.
With quirks of charm, they're truly grand,
A softness held in doodled hands.

So raise your glasses, toast the light,
To those who cry and laugh in flight.
In quirky love, let's all unite,
For sensitivity? A pure delight!

## Safe Harbor for Melancholy

In a harbor soft, where clouds drift by,
Melancholy sails under a heavy sky.
With a snack of cookies, not too sweet,
It finds a place where worries meet.

A boat of feelings, all a-churn,
Rocking gently, lessons learned.
With each wave, a laugh or sigh,
As seagulls cackle, oh my my!

The lighthouse beams a quirky glow,
To guide the heart through ebb and flow.
Boating snacks like chips and dip,
Who knew that sadness could taste like chips?

So anchor down, let troubles glide,
With humor as our trusty guide.
In these waters, let joy unfurl,
Where laughter meets the moody swirl!

## Whispers of Protection

In cozy nooks with blankets piled,
Whispers soften worries, all reviled.
A fort of pillows, laughter holds,
Where secrets bloom and fun unfolds.

With capes made from sheets, we save the day,
While giggling foes try to find a way.
The bravest souls with hearts so stout,
Can manage fears with shouts and clout.

The guardian's grin, a sight to behold,
With jokes that shimmy and lightly scold.
A shield of chuckles, silly and bright,
Wraps us snug, in soft delight.

So let the whispers fly and sway,
In lands where laughter finds its way.
With silly charms and friendly cheer,
We'll protect each other, year after year!

## Care for the Heart's Petals


In the garden of giggles, blossoms sway,
Petals of laughter brighten the gray.
Sprinkle some kindness, watch them unfold,
Whispering secrets, even the bold.

A cactus in love, oh what a sight,
Wearing a smile that's so full of light.
With humor as water, joy will ignite,
Watch out for thorns, they might take a bite!

Butterflies flutter, with winks and a tease,
Tickling the petals, swaying with ease.
In this floral dance, join the parade,
Grow wild with your laughter, let it cascade.

Embrace the chaos, let whimsy be found,
With the silliest jokes, we're all tightly bound.
In the pot of affection, sprinkle some cheer,
Care for the heart, let the fun persevere.

## Embracing Vulnerability

Oh, to be open, without a disguise,
Walking on tightropes, under strange skies.
Wobbly and giggly, we dance through the air,
Finding our balance, without a care.

When tears are just puddles, dive right in,
Splashing through silliness, let the fun begin.
A nervous giraffe, in a bowtie too bright,
Who knew vulnerability could be such a sight?

With ticklish confessions, we share our woes,
Bumbling through stories, a laughter arose.
In the land of the awkward, we twirl and we spin,
Finding warm comfort, where the fun can begin.

So shout out your secrets, sing loud and clear,
In the world of the real, let go of the fear.
A soft belly laugh, it's the best kind of shield,
Embrace every quirk, let your heart be revealed.

## Soothing the Delicate Spirit

A feathered friend with a quirky tune,
Sings silly sonnets by the light of the moon.
Dancing on breezes, so gentle, yet spry,
Whimsical whispers, as they float by.

Hats made of cotton candy, oh, what a sight!
Wearing smiles as they flutter, spreading delight.
Like a cupcake in sunshine, sweet and so bright,
Softening spirits with giggles in flight.

Bubbles unearthing the giggles within,
As we bounce through the meadows and spin.
Soothing the heart, like a plush teddy bear,
Wrap up your worries, let laughter be rare.

So here's to the delicate, who sway in the storm,
Embracing the softness, they'll weather the swarm.
With each little chuckle, we polish our art,
Soothing the spirit, straight from the heart.

## Cultivating Softness

In a field of soft pillows, we dream so wide,
Tickling our senses, with laughter as our guide.
Growing great giggles in every crevice,
A garden of kindness, oh so generous.

Sprouts of joy peek from beneath a shoe,
What a surprise, there's a joke coming through!
So let's brew some laughter, with silliness near,
Cultivate delight, from chuckles to cheer.

The soil is our jest, the rain drops our glee,
Planting the seeds of jubilation, you see.
With every sprout, there's a snicker or two,
In a patch so fluffy, it's absurd, but it's true.

Gather the smiles, let them blossom and flow,
Between every chuckle, let affection grow.
In this patch of softness, we find our sweet call,
Come play in the garden, quite funny for all!

## A Garden for the Delicate

In a patch of grass so fine,
Grew a flower who couldn't whine.
It danced when raindrops came to play,
But hid from sun, oh what a day!

A snail nearby would roam and sing,
To cheer the blooms with joy they'd bring.
The bees all buzzed, in tiny suits,
On the lookout for their morning fruits.

The daisies giggled, pink and bright,
As petals dressed in pure delight.
They laughed at weeds that tried to creep,
And shared their secrets, safe and deep.

But when the wind decided to toy,
Flower petals flew, oh what a joy!
The laughter echoed, round and round,
In a garden where mirth was found.

## **Cradled in Care**

A tiny plant in a teacup sat,
Wore a tiny hat, how about that?
It sipped on sunlight with a grin,
And danced in shadows, a real win!

A squirrel swung by with a cheeky chat,
Offering nuts and a friendly spat.
"Care for a nibble?" it cheerfully asked,
But the teacup plant had mischief tasked!

So it tickled the squirrel with leaves of green,
Turning a snack into a fun routine.
Together they spun, a whirlwind of cheer,
In a sheltered spot, no reason to fear.

Oh, the giggles that floated on air,
In a cozy world, filled with flair.
A place where joy could grow so tall,
In the kingdom of care, they ruled it all!

## Sowing Seeds of Kindness

With a sprinkle here and a sprinkle there,
We sowed some seeds with utmost care.
A giant carrot grew with a shout,
While radishes played hide and seek about.

The lettuce wore shades, looking cool,
While tomatoes splashed in a splashy pool.
Peppers did pirouettes, quite the scene,
In this garden of quirks, oh so keen!

But who knew kindness could grow so wide,
Leaving the grumpy cabbage to hide?
With every hearty laugh and cheer,
Sprouts of joy popped up everywhere near!

And when the harvest finally came,
All leafy friends played a silly game.
They tossed their veggies like a ball,
In this patch of love, there was space for all!

## The Soft Echo of Hope

A feather floated down from the sky,
Tickling a worm who was strolling by.
It laughed and giggled, what a delight,
In a world that seemed so very bright!

A butterfly flapped with colors galore,
Joining the worm in a dance to explore.
They twirled and spun, with grace and flair,
Inviting the daisies to join in the air.

With each gentle breeze came a whisper so sweet,
Carrying dreams on their tiny feet.
And as they rose with a spring in their hop,
The garden erupted, and never would stop!

So here in this garden, where laughter does bloom,
Echoes of hope fill every room.
With a wink and a twist, let the fun unfold,
In a place where stories of joy are told!

## Horizons of Hope

In the garden of dreams, we plant our seeds,
Watering with laughter, we fulfill our needs.
Sunshine and giggles, a light-hearted dance,
We'll bloom with a wink, given half a chance.

Underneath our hats, we stash silly jokes,
With every sprout, we share our pokes.
Fertilizer made of puns, nice and ripe,
Who knew that joy could have so much hype?

Growing together, we form quite a crew,
A patchwork of smiles in every hue.
Bumblebees buzzing, they laugh with us too,
Together we flourish, what a hullabaloo!

So let's sing to the skies and tickle the breeze,
Planting our glee with the utmost ease.
For where there's a chuckle, there's growth in the air,
In the garden of hope, there's always a flare.

**Sheltering the Vulnerable**

In a cozy nook, the shy squirrels hide,
Building a fortress, with peanuts inside.
With blankets of leaves and a warm, soft rug,
They turn their abode into a snug little hug.

The fearless raccoons bring snacks to the show,
While rabbits hop in with their own kind of flow.
They set up a feast with all things absurd,
Telling tall tales, flying like a bird.

Every critter gathers, they dance on their toes,
Whiskers twitching to the music that flows.
With each leaping laugh and a twirl in the shade,
They build their community, no plans to invade.

So join in the fun, with smiles to spare,
In this wacky retreat, you'll find friends everywhere.
For in silly shelters, we're all in the game,
Laughing and playing, it's our joyful name.

## Names of the Unsung

There's a turtle named Timothy, moves quite slow,
But his wisdom is golden, as he runs the show.
In a race with a hare, he'd make quite a scene,
While everyone cheers, 'It's a daring routine!'

Then we've got Fiona, the fish with a flair,
She wiggles and giggles, as she conquers the air.
With a splash in the pond, she's the queen of surprise,
Bringing bubbles of laughter that float to the skies.

Oh, don't forget Gerald, the gopher with style,
He digs like a champ, oh, he goes the extra mile!
With a smile and a wink, he's not one to miss,
His friends cheer him on, it's a wholesome bliss.

So raise up the banners for those who are shy,
In the tales they weave, we let our hearts fly.
For each name unsung holds a bashful pride,
In the quirky little tales, we all can abide.

## **Lanterns in the Dark**

When shadows loom near, and giggles fade out,
We gather our lanterns, with a flicker of doubt.
A parade of glowworms, each one a delight,
Wobbling through the night, they prepare for flight.

Each lantern's a laugh, a twinkle, a grin,
Conquering darkness, oh, let the fun begin!
With whispers and chuckles, they light up the night,
Creating a festival, so warm and bright.

Dancing in circles, they swirl like a breeze,
Chasing the shadows, with giggles that tease.
In the depths of the quiet, a cacophony thrives,
Through silliness shared, we feel so alive!

So let your glow shine, let your spirits embark,
In lantern-lit laughter, we'll ignite the spark.
For even in dark times, smile wide and bold,
With humor as our lantern, our stories unfold.

## Serenade for the Sensitive

Oh, dear soul, you've got it rough,
Life's a game, but you call it tough.
With a wink and a nudge, I'm here,
To sprinkle some laughter, bring you cheer.

When you feel like a wilting plant,
Just remember, even cacti can chant.
Let's dance in rain, not fear the mud,
A little joy grows in every bud.

With a tickle and a silly face,
Life's a whimsical, goofy race.
Grab a balloon, let worries float,
In this silly symphony, be the goat!

So here's to the gentle and the shy,
May your laughter soar, touch the sky.
With a heart so soft, you'll still take flight,
Playing this serenade, all day and night.

## The Warmth of a Gentle Touch

In a world where chaos reigns,
A soft touch feels like gentle trains.
Like a kitten's purr or a puppy's paw,
It's the magic secret they never saw.

With hugs that feel like warm, fresh bread,
And high-fives that dance in your head.
Let's pretend we're clouds, fluffy and light,
Drifting through giggles, oh what a sight!

A tickle fight waiting on the sand,
Is like giving your heart a helping hand.
With every pat, the worries fade,
Laughing so hard, decisions are made!

So come take a leap into this touch,
In a world that's heavy, it means so much.
Let's high-five the moon, below or above,
In this daily dance, let's twirl with love.

## Healing the Gentle Heart

Oh gentle heart, so easily pricked,
With every joke, let's get you licked.
Here's a bandage made of fun and cheer,
To patch the spots you hold so dear.

When worries bubble like gum on a shoe,
Let's pop them together—just me and you!
Float like a feather, fly in the breeze,
With every chuckle, we'll feel at ease.

Embrace the quirks, the odd little traits,
Dance through the storm, it's never too late.
With laughter's glue, we'll seal every crack,
Turning every frown to a silly knack.

So here's to healing, let's kick up our heels,
And make sure everyone here feels!
With a heart so gentle, so ready to play,
We'll mend it with giggles, hip-hip-hooray!

## **Nurtured by Love's Embrace**

Beneath the stars, where cuddles thrive,
We'll whip up a potion of giggles alive.
With every bear hug, warm and tight,
We nourish each smile 'til the morning light.

In the garden of friendship, let's plant some fun,
Water it daily till we're all spun.
With laughter as fertilizer, sunshine our guide,
Love grows wild on this wacky ride.

Whisk away sorrows with a sprinkle of spice,
A pinch of absurdity, that's our advice.
So let's make a cake, all covered in laughs,
With frosting of joy, we'll take our sweet baths!

Bask in the sunlight, let the silliness flow,
In the embrace of love, we'll all overflow.
So here's to the tender, with love and grace,
We'll bloom together, what a wild place!

www.ingramcontent.com/pod-product-compliance
Lightning Source LLC
Chambersburg PA
CBHW050307120526
44590CB00016B/2524